The Jacks
Book

The Jacks Book

by Sally Chabert

Photographs by John Bean
Illustrations by Matthew Fox

Workman Publishing
New York

Library of Congress Cataloging-in-Publication Data

Chabert, Sally.
    The jacks book / by Sally Chabert ;
photographs by John Bean ; illustrations by Matthew Fox.
       p. cm.
    Includes bibliographical references (p.) and
index.
    Summary: A how-to book of games with jacks,
including techniques, history, recipes, and trivia.
Includes a set of fourteen jacks and a ball.
    ISBN 0-7611-1627-3 (pbk. : alk. paper)
    1. Jacks (Game) Juvenile literature. [1. Jacks
(Game) 2. Games.] I. Bean, John, photographer, ill.
II. Fox, Matthew, ill. III. Title.
GV1216.C53 1999
796.2—dc21   99–13139 CIP

Workman Publishing Company, Inc.
708 Broadway
New York, NY 10003-9555

Manufactured in the United States of America

First Printing May 1999

10 9 8 7 6 5 4 3 2 1

Contents

Introduction

✦ ✦ ✦

Jacks is an amazing game. It's been played by millions of people, over thousands of years, in every part of the world. So what's the catch? Why is it so popular? It's because the game is so simple *and* so rewarding.

Jacks is a series of challenges. When you master one challenge, you can smile, feel good, and move on to the next level; if you mess up, you can start over and keep playing until you get it right.

It's an encouraging and engaging concept: Challenge, play, success; challenge, play, success; challenge, play, success.

It's also a very enduring concept.

Archaeologists believe that about 20,000 years ago, Cro-Magnon boys and girls (and their parents) were pretty good players. Not only was it a fun way to relax after a long day of hunting and gathering, it was probably a great way for them to improve hand-eye coordination.

Your parents and grand-parents and great-grand-parents probably played some version of *Jacks* when they were kids. But they may have called the game something different, like *Jackstones*, *Fivestones*, or *Dibs*. And instead of the pronged metal jacks you have, they may have used stones, seeds, cloth bags filled with rice or beans, or even the bones of animals.

Ask your relatives about *Jacks*. Or better yet, invite them to play a game or two with you. They may have some long-forgotten tricks to show off and some great stories to share. And it's always fascinating to hear about being a kid in a different time and a different place, right?

With this book you can play *all* of the current *and* historical variations within the *Jacks* family of games. You'll play some of the games with a ball and others without. You can play with the jacks that come with this book, or you can play with stones, fake knuckle-bones (recipe included, page 168), little cloth sacks filled with rice, seeds, or beans (instructions included, page 148), or real knucklebones (recipe included, page 171).

You can play many of the games by yourself *or* with others (some games are best played with four or five players). You can organize a neighborhood or school *Jacks* tournament and get lots of friends, classmates, even teachers and parents involved.

One of the great things about *Jacks* is that you don't need a lot of equipment or much space to play. You can play indoors on a smooth floor or outside on a smooth surface like cement.

You can carry the jacks around in your pocket or toss them in your backpack. You can play by yourself on a rainy day or with your friends at recess. You don't need to take lessons or wear special gear (no helmets required!). *Jacks* is cheap, portable, easy to learn, and, of course, really fun!

And best of all, since almost every kid in the world can play at least one of the *Jacks* games in this book, you can play with a new friend no matter where you live, no matter where in the world you might visit, and no matter what languages are being spoken. *Jacks* is the United Nations of games.

CHAPTER 1

Jacks Family Tree

✣ ✣ ✣

JACKS HISTORY

J*acks* is an ancient game. A really, really ancient game. Although archaeological evidence indicates that the game first originated in Asia, prehistoric caves in Kiev, Ukraine, have ancient drawings of people perfecting their stone-tossing version of this classic game.

Skara Brae is a preserved Stone Age village in Europe estimated to have been built in 2000–1500 B.C. Archaeologists

◀ *This detail of a 1560 painting by Peter Brueghel shows kids playing Knucklebones.*

have uncovered evidence that games similar to *Jacks* were played with the knucklebones of sheep or goats.

More than 2,500 years ago, the Greek poet Homer mentioned *astragaloi* in his epic poems *The Iliad* and *The Odyssey. Astragaloi* were goat knucklebones that were cube-shaped and marked on all four sides; they were frequently used by the ancient Greeks as fortune-telling devices and gambling tools, but their primary use

A c 300 B.C. terra-cotta statue of Greek girls playing knucklebones

was as jacks-like playing pieces. Paintings on ancient Greek vases portray both gods and humans playing games with the bones.

Many a Roman grown-up and kid whiled away a Saturday afternoon playing *Backgammon* (*Tabula*), *Chess* (*Latrunculi*), *Tic-Tac-Toe* (*Terni Lapilli*), and *Checkers* (*Calculi*). However, many historians believe that *Tali*, a version of *Knucklebones* learned from the Greeks, was their very favorite game. The Romans developed a fancier version of the game by using materials such as wood, marble, ivory, glass, and precious gems or metals to make their *tali*. A marble frieze, uncovered in the ruins of Pompeii, the Italian city destroyed by a volcano in about the year 80, portrays a group of women playing *Tali*.

The Romans introduced *Jacks* to many countries during their military campaigns, yet the game is also found to have developed on its own in other parts of the world, from Russia to Polynesia, places where Romans had not yet ventured.

Over the years and across the continents the game of *Jacks* has been called *Jackstones, Fivestones, Dibs, Chance Bone,* and *Knucklebones,* among many others. But why *"Jacks"*? Where did that word come from? Here goes: "Jacks" comes from "jackstones," which comes from "chackstones," which comes from "chalkstones," which are "stones to be tossed." Although people really should listen carefully and pronounce clearly, history's a lot more fun when words get mixed up.

Fast-forward hundreds of years: The children of American pioneers, as they traveled west in the 1800s, often played *Jacks.* It was the perfect travel game. All they needed were a few players, some chicken or turkey bones, and a small playing surface.

In the traditional American game of

An ancient Pompeiian drawing of Roman goddesses playing knucklebones.

Jacks, players would toss five or more counters or "jacks" into the air with one hand; they would then try to catch as many jacks as possible in the same hand, palm up or palm down.

In modern American *Jacks* games, a rubber ball is usually incorporated and the object is to pick up a certain number of six-pronged metal or plastic jacks. Each player takes a turn. The player first scatters the jacks on the floor and then tosses the ball in the air. While the ball bounces once the player must pick up the designated jacks and catch the ball before it bounces again. If the player misses any of these steps, it becomes the next player's turn. As you will see, there are lots of variables that can be added to make the game more challenging; the trick is to practice alone and then remain calm when competing (just like any game!).

UNITED NATIONS OF *JACKS*

J*acks* offers what other classic games cannot. It is *the* multicultural, multigenerational game. In some form, the game is played everywhere in the world, and has been since the dawn of humankind. Today, in Brazil, kids play *Cinco Marias* with stones. In Egypt, they use apricot seeds, while in Japan and China, kids use little cloth bags filled with rice. In New Zealand, children play *Huripapa* with the knucklebones of sheep.

Over the next few pages is a selection of the many countries—and their corresponding locations on a world map—in which some version of *Jacks* is played.

Do you have friends, relatives, or pen pals who live in any of these countries? If so, you could surprise them with a letter or e-mail about how you've been playing their version of *Jacks*. Then suggest that the next time you visit one another, you could both bring along jacks (or pebbles or beans or goat knee bones) and have an international tournament.

JACKS AROUND
THE WORLD

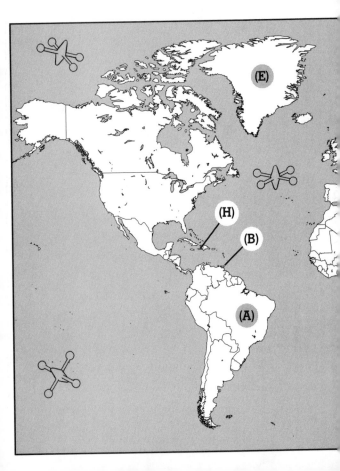

As you can see, *Jacks* games are played everywhere! Refer to pages 26 through 29 for the explanations of the labels shown below.

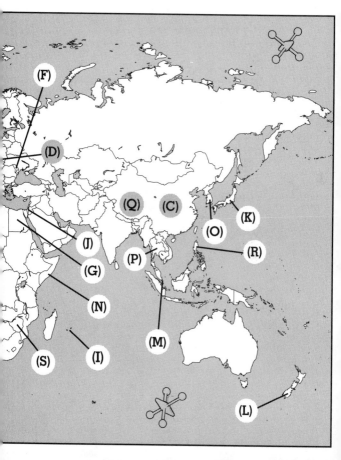

(A) Brazil—The game of *Cinco Marias* is played with small stones instead of jacks.

(B) Caribbean Islands of Trinidad and Tobago—The game of *Trier* is played with five stones or beans.

(C) China—On mainland China, where the game of *Jacks* is believed to have originated, one version of *Jacks*, known as *Zhua San* (page 126), is played with stones.

(D) The Czech Republic—Six small, smooth seeds, or pebbles, are used for a popular and traditional game (page 56, *Czech Jacks*).

(E) Greenland—Eskimos play a game using the small finger bones of seal flippers.

(F) Eastern Europe—Using five bones, girls play the traditional game of *Ghop Bagi*.

(G) Egypt—Children use apricot seeds in a game whose object is to gather the most seeds.

(H) Haiti—Haitian children use goat knuckles to play the game of *Osselets* (page 88).

(I) Island of Mauritius, Indian Ocean—Children enjoy a *Knucklebones* game (page 140) in which the objective is to have the largest number of pebbles at the end of the playing period.

(J) Israel—*Hamesh Avanim* (page 122) is played with five gold-colored cubes.

(K) Japan—The game of *Otedama* (page 72) is played with small cloth bags filled with rice.

(L) New Zealand—Long before European settlers arrived, the native Maori were playing the game of *Huripapa* (page 84) with seeds.

(M) Singapore—The popular game of *Five Sacks* (page 106) resembles juggling and is played with small sacks of rice.

(N) Somalia—The game of *Garir* (page 95), played with stones, requires digging a shallow hole in the ground.

(O) South Korea—*Kong-Keui* (page 79) is played with stones in three rounds called "laying the eggs," "setting the eggs," and "hatching the eggs."

(P) Thailand—The very popular game of *Maakgep* (page 143) is played with stones.

(Q) Tibet—*Abhadho* (pages 135), a series of games closely resembling *Jacks*, is played with the knee bones of goats.

(R) Vietnam—Vietnamese children play a game called *Truyen-Truyen* (page 115) with chopsticks and a ball.

(S) Zimbabwe—Around the edge of a shallow hole, a version of *Jacks* called *Iguni* (page 102) is played with twelve smooth, round pebbles, small enough to all be held in one hand.

Kids play Jacks *or* Jacks-*style games all over the world.*

CHAPTER 2

Jackspertise

✤ ✤ ✤

So you want to be a *Jacks* expert? The basic rules of *Jacks* are simple and quite easy to learn, so there's no need to memorize complicated instructions. The guidelines and helpful hints that follow over the next several pages are all you need to be on your way to "Jackspertise." If you get confused during any of the games, or if you have a rules dispute with an opponent, you can always turn back to this chapter and settle any questions. If you need any extra help or skill-building hints, you can also refer back to this chapter. Don't be embarrassed to review the basics; it's how amateurs become professionals!

DOS AND DON'TS: THE BASIC RULES

There are many versions of the game of *Jacks* and the number of jacks used varies for each, but today, most games are played with ten or six jacks and a small rubber ball. (This book's set comes with fifteen jacks and one ball. So if you really want to challenge yourself you can use all fifteen. Or, just fill in with the extra jacks if you lose any.)

The basic rules noted here apply to every game in this book *unless the directions say otherwise*.

• You can use only one hand for picking up jacks and tossing the ball or jacks.

• You can touch only the jacks you're trying to pick up, even if they're stuck in a pile with other jacks. However, the more you play, the better you'll get at tossing the jacks just right—so they are not clumped together yet they're close enough to one another to be picked up conveniently.

• If you're using a ball, and it bounces more than once in a play or you don't catch it, you lose your turn.

• If you drop a picked up jack or pick up the wrong number of jacks you lose your turn.

• You have to pick up the correct number of jacks. If you're playing *Threesies*, for example, you must pick up three jacks at a time—no more, no less.

• In a round with leftover jacks, you scoop up any remaining jacks all at once. If you're using ten jacks and playing *Sevensies*, pick up seven jacks on one toss of the ball and then pick up the remaining three jacks on the next toss.

• If you're playing a game in rounds, all the way from *Onesies* to *Tensies*, for example, and you make a mistake or "commit a foul," you don't go all the way back to *Onesies* on your next turn. Start instead at whichever round you committed the foul. Failure to begin a turn at the correct round will cost you another turn, so pay attention!

• *Jacks* is best played squatting or sitting on a smooth floor, a low-pile rug, or smooth cement.

• You must sit in the same place and position for the whole game; so get comfortable before you begin.

EQUIPMENT

With your set of fifteen jacks and the small bouncing ball, you can play any game in this book. One set of jacks and a ball can be shared by all players. If you find yourself without your set of jacks, you can always use dice, pebbles from the board game of Go, or small, smooth stones. Most of the international games are traditionally played with found or homemade playing pieces, such as stones, seeds, nuts, or knucklebones. For these games you can use your jacks or the traditional playing pieces—whichever you like.

JACKS-O-RaMA

Fancy American jacks.

"Fake" knucklebones (see page 168).

Rice sacks from Japan (see page 148).

Real knucklebones (see page 171).

Traditional American jacks.

HOW MANY PLAYERS?

That's up to you! Alone? Bored? Play by yourself! It's a good way to improve your skills while no one's watching.

But *Jacks* is also a great game to play with others. Two or three players are ideal. Although you can play all of these *Jacks* games with an additional three or four players, you'll spend a lot of time just waiting for your turn.

Be sure to check out the game Jackstones (page 66). It's best when played with at least eight players!

IMPORTANT!
DEFINITION DUO!

I t'll be a lot easier to enjoy and use this book if you first learn two simple words that are used in many of the game instructions. Ask somebody to begin bouncing your *Jacks* ball while you read this page. Before the ball has been bounced even twenty times, you'll know what these two words mean. Try it!

Jackstone—In almost all games of *Jacks*, an object is thrown in the air while other items are quickly scooped up. Usually, a ball is tossed, but stones, jacks, and even seeds are sometimes tossed. Whatever it is, the tossed item is known as the "jackstone."

Scatter—Most rounds of *Jacks* begin with the player tossing some number of things (jacks, seeds, or stones) on the ground. To toss or throw these things on the ground is to "scatter" them.

WHO GOES FIRST?

When playing *Jacks* with your friends, you'll always need to decide who goes first. There are two ways to determine this, and they've both been popular among *Jacks* players for generations.

Flipping—One by one, each player takes the same number of jacks in one hand, tosses them a couple of inches into the air, flips over the same hand, and tries to catch as many jacks as possible on the back of that hand.

The player who catches the most jacks goes first. If anyone ties, flip again.

If you want to try an easier version, use the two-part two-handed flip.

Hold your jacks with your hands
together, palms up, as if you're offer-
ing them to someone. Toss the jacks,
turn your hands over, palms down,
bring the backs of your hands together,
and catch as many jacks as you can.
From the back of your hands, toss the
jacks again. Turn over your hands,
cup them again, and catch as many
jacks as possible.

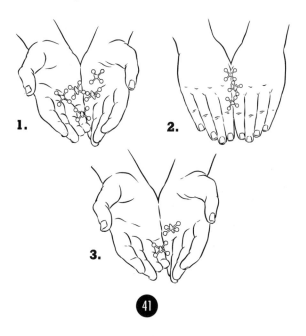

1.

2.

3.

Rock, Paper, Scissors—This only works for two or three players. Lift your fists in the air, bring them down, call "rock," raise your fists again, bring them down, call "paper," raise your fists again, bring them down, call "scissors." But on this third round, each player makes a sign for either rock (fist), paper (flat hand), or scissors (index and third finger pointing out). Rocks can "break" scissors (rock wins). Scissors can "cut" paper (scissors win). Paper can "cover" rock (paper wins). The player who wins goes first. If two or more people make the same sign, have a "shoot-out" to break the tie.

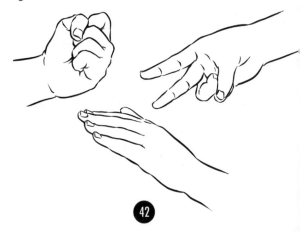

HELPFUL HINTS

Throwing the Ball—Throw the ball *high* (so that you have plenty of time to pick up the jacks) and *straight* (so that it bounces for an easy catch), but not so *hard* that it flies away, out of control.

Tossing the Jacks—If you're playing to pick up just one or two jacks at a time (like *Onesies* or *Twosies*), toss the jacks so that they land with lots of space between them. That way, it's easier not to touch the other jacks by mistake. But if you're playing to pick up lots of jacks (like *Ninesies* or *Tensies*), toss the jacks so that they land close enough together to be easily picked up on one toss of the ball.

When You Don't Need the Ball—If a game uses a jack or stone instead of a ball as your jackstone (the thing you toss, remember?), you'll be instructed to first scatter the stones or jacks. Then you'll have to pick one of them to be your jackstone. Here's the helpful hint: Look carefully at the tossed jacks or stones. If one jack is interlocked with another, or one jack or stone is so close to others that it would be hard to remove without moving the others, choose one of those as your jackstone. Likewise, if a scattered jack or stone is so far away from the others that it's going to be difficult to pick it up, choose that one as your jackstone.

If you choose to play certain games with small stones (about the size of, or a little bigger than, your thumbnail) instead of your jacks, be sure to choose the largest of your stones as the jackstone. This will make your task of picking up the smaller stones easier.

Blow Out!—If your tossed ball lands on a jack and goes flying off on a weird bounce (just as a car might swerve off in an odd direction if one of its tires blew out), yell "Blow out!" before any of your opponents do, and you can toss the ball again. Note: Adding "Blow out!" to the game is up to you and your friends. It is not one of the standard rules for traditional *Jacks* games.

Games Too Easy?—Okay, that happens. So try this: When you scatter the jacks in any of the games, make a rule that each jack has to be at least a hand's width apart from every other jack. If not, you have to scatter the jacks again. If after your second scattering, they're still not a hand's width apart, you lose your turn.

In General—Get a good night's sleep, exercise regularly, and minimize your intake of high-caffeine soda (the stuff makes your hands shake—not a good attribute for a star *Jacks* player).

The Games

✧ ✧ ✧

Here you go! At last! Enough of the rules and regulations—let the games begin! As you discover, enjoy, and master the many different games that follow, don't be surprised if you find yourself marveling at the simple activity they all share: toss something, do something, catch something. Good luck, and remember the first and most important *Jacks* rule of all: have fun!

Onesies

What you need: **ball, 10 jacks**

This is *the* game. The original. The granddaddy of all other *Jacks* games. So it's a good idea to learn and master this one first.

1. Gather the ten jacks in one hand and scatter them on the playing surface with one toss.

2. Toss the ball in the air, pick up one jack, let the ball bounce *once*, and catch the ball with the *same* hand. Transfer the jack you just picked up to the other hand.

3. Repeat step 2 with another jack and keep repeating until all the jacks are picked up and held in your nonthrowing hand.

4. Remember, if you drop the ball, or let it bounce twice, or drop a jack, or move any jack other than the one you're trying to pick up, your turn is over.

5. The first player to gather all the jacks in one turn, without messing up, wins.

Twosies, Threesies, etc.

What you need: **ball, 10 jacks**

Twosies, *Threesies, Foursies, Fivesies, Sixsies, Sevensies, Eightsies, Ninesies,* and *Tensies* are all extensions of the *Onesies* game you've mastered by now.

Just to make life easier, so that there is no need to list all these games

Reminder: See page 40 if you need help deciding who goes first.

49

whenever they are mentioned, this book sometimes refers to this *"-sies"* branch of the *Jacks* family as *"Onesies, Twosies,* and *So-Onsies."*

You can play these as individual games—"Let's play *Threesies!*" or "Let's play *Fivesies!*"—or you can play these as rounds in a larger game, like this:

1. Begin by playing *Onesies*.

2. Once you've successfully completed *Onesies*, start all over again, but this time pick up two jacks at a time. This is called *Twosies*.

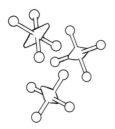 **3.** Once you've success-fully picked up all the jacks by twos *(Twosies)*, start all over again, but this time pick up three jacks at a time. This is called *Threesies*.

4. See a pattern developing here? Good—go with it! Keep repeating the pattern until you've gotten all the way to *Tensies*. *Tensies* is a fun one. Think about it. You've got to throw the ball, pick up *all* ten jacks, and catch the ball after one bounce with the *same* hand. Phew!

5. The first player to complete all of the rounds, up to and including *Tensies* wins.

• • • • • • • • • • • • • • • • • •

Haystacks

Haystacks are when two jacks are stacked on top of each other. Some people like to add this rule to a *Jacks* game: If you holler "haystacks" before anyone else does, you can separate the two jacks before tossing your ball.

• • • • • • • • • • • • • • • • • •

Double Bounce

What you need: **ball, 10 jacks**

This game is played just like *Onesies*, *Twosies*, and *So-Onsies* but get a load of this: The ball must bounce *twice* before it is caught—so throw it high!

1. Gather the ten jacks in one hand and scatter them on the playing surface with one toss.

2. Toss the ball in the air, pick up one jack, let the ball bounce *twice*, and catch the ball with the *same* hand. Put the jack you just picked up in your other hand.

3. Repeat step 2 with another jack and keep repeating until all the jacks are picked up and held in your non-throwing hand.

4. Don't forget, you must let the ball bounce twice. And if you drop the ball, or drop a jack, or move any jack other than the one you're trying to pick up, your turn is over.

5. The first player to gather all the jacks wins.

No Bounce

What you need: **ball, 10 jacks**

This game is played just like *Onesies, Twosies,* and *So-Onsies* but check this out: You must pick up a jack and catch the ball *before* it bounces (hard to do, so toss the ball high!).

1. Gather the ten jacks in one hand and scatter them with one toss.

2. Toss the ball in the air, pick up one jack, and catch the ball *before* it bounces, all with the *same* hand. Put the jack you just picked up in your other hand.

3. Repeat step 2 with another jack and keep repeating until all the jacks are picked up and held in your nonthrowing hand.

4. If you drop the ball, or let it bounce, or drop a jack, or move any jack other than the one you're trying to pick up, your turn is over.

5. The first player to gather all the jacks wins.

• •

Record Numbers

Gather together all your friends and their jacks. See how far you can push this *Onesies, Twosies,* and *So-Onsies* thing. How many jacks do you have all together? Forty-six? Can you play *Forty-sixsies?* Just how many jacks can your hand hold? Go for it! Better yet, gather up pen pals and far-flung relatives and their jacks. Can you play *Five-hundred-and-seventy-eightsies?* Is it time to contact *The Guinness Book of World Records?*

• •

Czech Jacks

What you need: **ball, 6 jacks (or seeds)**

In the Czech Republic, kids play a version of the classic *Jacks* game using six seeds, and perform each play first with the right hand, then with the left.

For example, on *Onesies* you would throw the ball with your right hand and pick up a jack with the same hand. Next, you would throw the ball with your left hand and pick up a jack with the same hand. And then you'd go back to the right hand for the next play, and so on.

This is a great way to increase your dexterity!

Eggs in the Basket

What you need: **ball, 10 jacks**

This game is played just like *Onesies, Twosies,* and *So-Onsies,* but with one little twist: the old switcheroo!

1. Gather the ten jacks in your usual playing hand and scatter them on the playing surface with one toss. (You'll want the jacks to be fairly well separated.)

2. Cup the palm of your other hand into a little "basket."

3. Toss the ball, pick up an "egg" (a jack), and *place it in the basket* (your other hand) while the ball bounces just once. This one added step can make this game a lot more difficult and a lot more fun. Set the egg aside to empty your basket after you've caught the ball.

4. Continue until all of the jacks are picked up. Don't be discouraged if this game is difficult at first—you'll get better!

Just remember, the ball can only bounce once.

5. You can play all the way through *Tensies*.

Now, to make this game even *more* difficult, try to do the "Bulging Basket": Keep each egg you pick up in your "basket" hand; don't empty the basket between pickups. By the end of the round, you'll be trying to cram a tenth egg into your basket. Can you do it?

Sweeps

What you need: **ball, 6 jacks**

Sweeps is similar to the games of *Onesies*, *Twosies*, and *So-Onsies* but before picking up the jacks, will you:

    a. wish them in close to your body?
    b. blow them in close to your body?
    c. sweep them in close to your body?*

1. Gather the six jacks in one hand and scatter them on the playing surface with one toss.

2. Toss the ball in the air with one hand, and while it bounces just once, place the fingers of the same hand on one jack. Without lifting the jack

---

* Of course! The answer is c: sweep them in close to your body.

from the playing surface, sweep it across the surface until it's close to your body.

3. Then pick up the swept jack and catch the bounced ball with the same hand. Warning: This "sweep" adds a step that makes the game much more difficult than you may think.

4. Sweep all the jacks one by one; then rescatter and proceed sweeping by twos, then by threes, and so on, through *Sixsies*.

Horsie

What you need: **5 jacks (or stones)**

Horsie is a good basic skill builder. Play this game and you're sure to develop your flipping and catching skills.

Put all five jacks in the palm of your playing hand. Toss all five jacks in the air and try to catch them on the back of the same hand. Now toss those jacks off the back of your hand, flip your hand, and try to catch them all in your palm. If you're competing, the winner in *Horsie* is the player who has the most jacks in his or her hand after the second flip.

Pigs in the Pen

What you need: **ball, 10 jacks**

This game is like *Onesies*, but with a barnyard challenge. Instead of picking up the jacks, you *corral* them, like barnyard pigs, into a pen.

1. Gather the ten jacks in one hand and scatter them on the playing surface with one toss. (Try to get some decent space between each one.)

2. Place your nonthrowing, nonscooping, noncatching hand on the playing surface so that your fingertips, thumb, and wrist touch the surface to form a little pen for the jacks.

Once you've formed your pen, it must stay put—you can't move it around. Not at all.

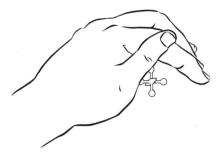

3. Toss the ball in the air, push a "pig" (a jack) into the "pen," and catch the ball after one bounce. You can lift the thumb and forefinger of your pen from the playing surface to let the pig in, but the rest of your hand can't move. If you drop the ball or leave any jacks outside the pen, it's a "miss"—you lose your turn.

4. Continue by putting pigs into the pen by twos, then by threes, all the way through *Tensies*.

5. The first player to get all ten pigs in the pen at once is the winner!

Pigs over the Fence

What you need: **ball, 10 jacks**

Pigs over the Fence is very similar to *Pigs in the Pen*, but instead of building a pen, you use your nonplaying hand to make a simple fence by placing your hand at a right angle to the playing surface. In this game, instead of corralling your pigs in the pen, you jump them over the fence.

1. Scatter all ten jacks on the playing surface with one toss. (You'll want to get a bit of space between each one.)

2. Place your nonthrowing, nonscooping, noncatching hand on the playing surface at a right angle to make a simple fence.

Once you've formed your fence, it
must stay put—you can't move it around.

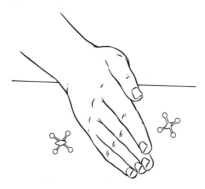

3. Toss the ball in the air, pick up a
"pig" (a jack), place it on the other
side of the "fence," and catch the ball
after one bounce. If you drop the ball,
miss the ball, drop a jack, or miss a
jack, you lose your turn.

4. Continue by putting pigs over the
fence by twos, then by threes.

5. The first player to get all ten pigs
over the fence at once is the winner!

Jackstones

What you need: **10 to 15 jacks for each player (or use peach or plum pits, almonds, or other nuts of similar size).**

Many variations of *Jacks* are called *Jackstones*. This version is popular with children in the East African country of Kenya, where they play the game with nuts from the African palm tree. One of the really neat things about this game is that it is best played with a crowd of ten or more players!

1. The players should put all of their jacks *but one* into a big central pile and then sit in a circle around the pile. The jack that each player keeps is his or her jackstone.

2. When it's your turn, toss your jackstone in the air. Use your tossing hand to reach into the pile, grab as many jacks as you can, and catch the jack-stone before it hits the floor.

3. If you drop any of the jacks or don't catch your jackstone, you must put all your jacks back in the pile (even the ones you may have already won.)

4. Continue around the circle until all the jacks are gone. The player with the most jacks at the end of the game is the winner.

Match the Jacks

1. Jack Benny

A. a playing card

2. jack-in-the-box

B. U.S. President, 1960–1963

3. blackjack

C. late-night talk show pioneer

4. Jack Russell

D. actor, *As Good As It Gets*

5. jumping jack

E. a card game, aka "twenty-one"

6. Billy Jack

F. a classic fairy tale

7. flapjacks

G. an old-time comedian

8. John F. (Jack) Kennedy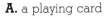

H. a notorious British murderer

9. jack

I. top prize winnings

10. Jack the Ripper

J. a very handy person

11. jackknife

12. Union Jack

13. Jack Paar

14. Jack London

15. "Jack and the Beanstalk"

16. jackrabbits

17. Jack Nicholson

18. jackpot

19. *Jacks*

20. jack-of-all-trades

K. the topic of this book

L. a rebellious film character, popular in the 1970s

M. hare-ish animals

N. a bouncy exercise

O. a dive or a weapon

P. pancakes

Q. a classic pop-up toy

R. the British flag

S. a breed of dog

T. author, *The Call of the Wild*

Answers: 1. G; 2. O; 3. E; 4. S; 5. N; 6. L; 7. P; 8. B; 9. A; 10. H; 11. O; 12. R; 13. C; 14. T; 15. F; 16. M; 17. D; 18. I; 19. K; 20. J

Crack the Eggs

What you need: **ball, 10 jacks**

In *Eggs in the Basket*, you thought of the jacks as eggs and treated them with great care. Now is your chance to recklessly crack 'em!

1. Gather the ten jacks in one hand and scatter them on the playing surface with one toss.

2. Toss the ball in the air. Now here's the catch: While the ball bounces once, you pick up a jack, "crack" it by tapping it on the floor, and catch the ball with the jack still in your hand!

3. Place the jack in the other hand and continue to pick up and crack the other jacks one at a time. Any ball or jack(s) drops or misses, and you lose your turn.

4. You can play
this all the way
through *Tensies*.
If you're playing
any of the *So-O*
"crack" your wh
handful-of
at once, n
at a time.

• •

Overs!

**Some *Jacks*-playing friends want to help
each other so much that they add this option
to their games: If you don't like the way you
scattered your jacks, just yell "Overs!" and
you can toss them again.**

• •

O_tedama

What you need: **9 small jacks bags (see directions on page 148, or use your jacks instead)**

The game of *Otedama* originated in Japan. The word *Otedama* comes from *te*, which means "hand," and *dama*, which means "ball." This game is similar to our traditional game of *Jacks*.

But for this game, it's fun to make and use your own jacks bags filled with rice. Be sure to make nine bags, eight of one color cloth and the ninth of a different color. This ninth bag will be your jackstone.

1. Toss the nine bags in the air, and catch only the jackstone. Let the others fall to the playing surface. If you miss the jackstone, you lose your turn.

2. Toss the jackstone bag in the air, pick up one of the other bags, and catch the jackstone bag again. Switch the picked-up bag to your nonthrowing hand. Repeat until all bags have been picked up.

3. Do *Twosies*, *Threesies*, and *Foursies*.

4. The player who first completes *Foursies* is the winner.

Trust

What you need: **ball, 10 jacks**

One of the great things about *Jacks* games is that they are most enjoyable when played with good and trusted friends. So how about a game that is as much based on trust and friendship as it is on the bounce of a ball, the luck of a toss, or the size of one's palms? This is that game.

You'll notice that *Trust* is very much like *Onesies* except that your success is based on a trusted friend's performance.

1. Have a friend gather the ten jacks in one hand and scatter them on the playing surface with one toss.

2. Your friend now tosses the ball in the air . . . BUT *you* pick up one jack, let

Are your friends Trust-worthy?

the ball bounce *once*, and catch the ball with the *same* hand. Transfer the jack you just picked up to your other hand.

3. Repeat step 2 with another jack and keep repeating until all the jacks are picked up and held in your noncatching hand.

4. Remember, if you drop the ball, or let it bounce twice, or drop a jack, or move any jack other than the one you're trying to pick up, your turn is over and your friend's turn begins.

5. The first player to gather all the jacks in one turn, without messing up, wins.

What's really special about this game is that no matter who wins in the end, the victory is due to both players (friends).

• •

Knucklebone Jack

Native Americans play a game using the knee bone of a cow or sheep. The bone is held between the thumb and the forefinger; the hand is quickly turned in a counterclock-wise motion; and the bone is released as the hand turns. Scoring is determined by where the bone falls.

• •

Tossless and Scatterfree

What you need: **5 jacks (or stones)**

Tossless and Scatterfree is a real change of pace—nothing is tossed or scattered! And if you're having trouble on the "pick-up" part of your game, this is a great skill builder.

1. Place four jacks at the corner of any imaginary rectangle. You can use a sheet of paper or a magazine to determine the size of the rectangle.

2. Place a fifth jack on the back of your "pick-up" hand.

3. Don't let that fifth Jack fall off your hand as you pick up—with the same hand—the four jacks, one after the other, holding them against the palm of your hand until all four are in this hand and the fifth still on top.

If any of the gathered jacks fall out, or if the jack on the back of your hand slides off, you lose your turn.

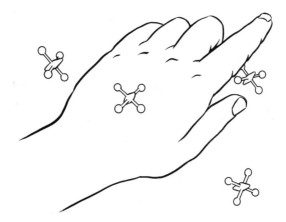

Kong-Keui

What you need: **5 jacks (or stones)**

In South Korea, *Kong-Keui* is a game traditionally played by boys with stones or pieces of brick. Girls play a version of this game with coins. The game involves three increasingly difficult rounds: "laying the eggs," "setting the eggs," and "hatching the eggs."

1. First scatter four jacks on the floor.

2. Toss the fifth jack (the jackstone) in the air, pick up one jack, and catch the jackstone.

3. Set the picked-up jack on the ground next to your nonthrowing hand. To complete the first round, repeat until all the "eggs" are "laid."

4. Now, place your nonthrowing hand palm down on the floor next to the four "laid eggs." Cup your palm a little so that you will be able to slide the "eggs" underneath.

5. Toss the fifth jack with your throwing hand, push one of the other jacks under your palm—hurry up!—and catch the tossed jack.

6. Keep throwing the fifth jack and moving the others until all the "eggs" are "set" under your palm. (You're one busy chicken!)

7. Now, take the "eggs" out from under your palm and place three of them on the ground in front of you.

8. Place the fourth jack against the inside of the little finger of your throwing hand. Curl your little finger around the jack so that you're holding it.

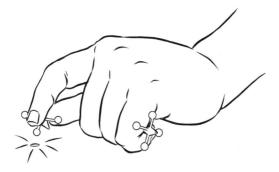

9. Throw the fifth jack, tap one of the jacks on the ground (keep that jack securely held in your little finger!), and catch the thrown jack. Phew!

10. Continue until all three jacks are tapped ("hatched").

11. The winner is the first player to complete all three rounds.

Rounding Up the Horses

What you need: **ball, 4 jacks**

Rounding up the Horses is a much fancier version of Pigs in the Pen. It should be; your average horse lives a much fancier life than your average pig.

1. Scatter the four jacks, or "horses," on the playing surface with one toss.

2. Place your nonthrowing hand, palm down, on the playing surface, and spread your thumb and fingers apart to create four "stalls."

3. Toss the ball, flick a horse into a stall, and catch the ball. Repeat with each horse, one horse to a stall.

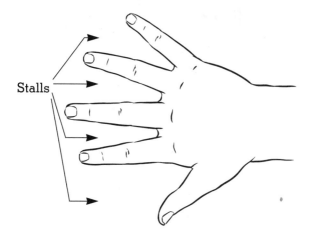

Stalls

4. After all the horses are in their stalls, flick them back out, one at a time. Toss the ball, flick a horse, and catch the ball after a single bounce.

5. The first player to move all the horses into the stalls and back out again is the winner.

Polly Put the Kettle On

What you need: **5 jacks (or knuckle-bones*)**

Long before European settlers arrived in New Zealand, the native Maori were playing the game of *Huripapa*, using peach pits or the knucklebones of sheep. *Polly Put the Kettle On* is one of many variations of *Huripapa*.

1. Scatter all five jacks.

2. Pick one of the jacks as your jackstone.

* You can play this game with your own "fake" knuckle-bones (see directions on page 168) or your own "real" knucklebones (see directions on page 171). Do you find the game easier to play with jacks or knuckle-bones? What do your friends think?

3. Toss the jackstone, move one of the four jacks next to another at an angle (they should be touching), and catch the jackstone.

4. Throw the jackstone again, move a third jack next to the others so that it touches them both, and catch the jackstone. You should now have a "burner": a tightly formed triangle of three jacks (imagine it as a burner on your family's kitchen stove).

5. The winner is the first player to place the kettle (the fourth jack) on top of the burner, without "burning" himself or herself on the burner (disrupting the other three jacks).

Now you're cookin'!

Downhill Racing

What you need: **ball, 10 jacks**

If you're looking for the near-ultimate *Jacks* challenge, try this game on a steep sidewalk or driveway. Just don't accidentally fold your legs into your chest, wrap your arms around them, tuck in your head, and suddenly roll down the hill like a runaway *Jacks* ball! Be careful!

• • • • • • • • • • • • • • • • • • • •

Hands Off, Buster!

You can add this fun little twist to any *Jacks* game if you and your friends are in the mood. Let's say that when you scatter your jacks some land really close to another player. If that player yells "Hands off, buster!" and you touch that player while trying to pick up the jacks, you lose your turn.

• • • • • • • • • • • • • • • • • • • •

Play this like *Onesies, Twosies,* all the way through *Tensies.*

1. Gather and scatter all ten jacks, then toss the ball as usual.

2. Pick up your jack(s) as the ball bounces, then catch the ball, again as usual.

3. Then—now pay attention!— let the ball roll away from you on the ground, put the jack(s) in your other hand, and catch the ball again before it gets out of reach.

See how a slanted surface can really change the nature of a *Jacks* game?

Osselets

What you need: **ball, 5 jacks (or osselets)**

The children of Haiti enjoy playing *Osselets* outdoors, all year round. *Osselets* (pronounced oo-SLAY) is another name for animal knuckles (you can make your own; just follow the directions on pages 168 and 171.)

Osselets is played just like *Onesies*, *Twosies*, and *So-Onsies* except for a pretty neat twist at the beginning of the game.

1. To begin, hold the ball and all five jacks in your throwing hand.

2. Toss both the ball and the jacks into the air and catch the ball before it bounces twice. Allow the jacks to scatter on the ground.

3. Toss the ball again, let it bounce only once, and pick up a jack.

4. Toss the ball again, keeping the first jack in your hand. Now pick up a second jack and catch the ball after the first bounce, all with the same hand.

5. Keep playing until you've picked up all five jacks one by one. The winner is the first player to have picked up all five jacks without any misses or any drops.

• •

Fun For the Whole Family

During the 1930s, in the Mediterranean resort area known as the Riviera, butchers cut, cured, and even colored knucklebones for the game of the same name. Lamb knee bones were used by children and women, and the larger sheep bones were used by men. Called osselets, they were often sold in toy stores in sets of five in a box.

• •

Loop de Loop

What you need: **5 jacks (or stones)**

Getting bored? Looking for something a little different? A *lot* different? Here you go, this has just got to be it: a jacks obstacle course.

1. Place four of the jacks in a line with several inches of space between them, like this:

2. Toss the fifth jack (the jackstone). Before you catch the jackstone, you must pick up one of the jacks on either end of the line and weave it in and out of the line, forming a triple loop

through the other jacks, as illustrated.
The goal is to trace the whole pattern.

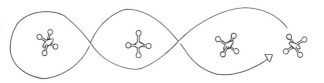

Your picked up jack can touch the
ground, but not any of the other jacks.
Leave the picked up jack wherever you
stop forming your loop when it's time
to catch the jackstone.

If you drop the jackstone, touch any
of the other jacks, or fail to complete
the entire pattern, you lose your turn.

3. The first player to complete the
loop wins.

Warning: This game might make
you feel a little loopy.

Five Finger Jacks

What you need: **6 jacks**

Whew! In need of some rest? A bit exhausted from all this *Jacks* play? Then *Five Finger Jacks* is the game for you! One of your hands is expected to do nothing but sit there. It's like one-hand nap time.

And if your *Jacks* ball is equally weary, that's even better! Because your *Jacks* ball also sits out this popular game.

1. Determine who goes first by *reverse* alphabetical order of each player's first name.

2. With one hand, toss six jacks onto the floor. Then pick up one to be your jackstone.

3. If you're right-handed, place your left hand—palm down, fingers spread wide—on the floor. Now send your left hand into a deep sleep. For the rest of the game it cannot move. It just sits there, resting, with its fingers spread wide. (Place your right hand on the floor if you're left-handed.)

4. With your right hand, toss the jack-stone into the air. While it's up there floating around, move one of your scat-

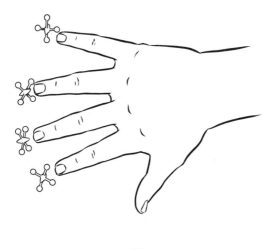

tered jacks to the tip of any finger on your left hand. Then catch the tossed jack with your right hand before it hits the floor.

5. Do it again. Toss the jackstone, move another one of the scattered jacks to the tip of another finger, and catch the jackstone before it hits the floor.

6. Repeat this move until you have a jack next to each fingertip.

7. Now, the biggie. Toss the jackstone one last time and—without moving your left hand—scoop up all five of the fingertip jacks and catch the jackstone before it hits the floor.

8. Any mistake at any step and it's back to the beginning. That's it.

Garir

What you need: **1 ball (or jackstone), 12 jacks (or stones)**

Because this game from the East African country of Somalia involves digging a shallow (1-inch-deep and 3-inch-wide) hole in the ground, it is better played outside than on your grandmother's heirloom rug.

And get a load of this: In Somalia, if you're walking along the street and see a potential *Jacks* opponent, you can yell out "Garir!" to secure the first turn. Really!

Another neat thing: in *Garir*, you're

allowed to touch and move *any* jacks—
not only those you're trying to pick up.

1. Dig a shallow hole in the ground just
big enough to hold the twelve jacks.
Put all twelve jacks in the hole.

2. Toss your ball in the air, take one
jack from the hole, and catch the ball
in the same hand. Put the picked up
jack aside. Do not let the ball bounce.

3. Continue removing the jacks, one
by one, until the hole is empty.

4. Then play *Twosies*: Take out two
jacks at a time.

5. Finally, play *Threesies*. Whoever is
the first to finish *Threesies* without any
drops or misses, wins.
   After the game is over, be sure to fill
up that hole before somebody named
Jack trips over it.

Jacks to the Rooftop

What you need: **7 jacks**

When you think about it, most *Jacks* games sound pretty reckless. Terms like "tossing," "scattering," "throwing," and "flipping" are often used, conveying a careless or even dangerous sensibility.

But not this *Jacks* game. *Jacks to the Rooftop* is perfect for the deliberate, organized, and focused "A-to-Z" sort of player. The jacks are arranged in a line, which you should think of as a ladder (how else are you going to get to the rooftop?).

You will not need your *Jacks* ball for this game. A mixture of balls and ladders is just too dangerous!

1. *Carefully* place six jacks on the playing surface, *neatly* lining them up like steps on a ladder. *Deliberately* leave a space about four fingertips wide between each jack.

2. *Cautiously* toss the seventh jack in the air. Use the index finger of your tossing hand to *meticulously* jump over the first jack of the ladder. Then catch the tossed jack before it hits the playing surface. *Cautiously* toss the

jack again. *Meticulously* jump over the second jack of the ladder. *Deliberately* catch the tossed jack.

3. Continue with this pattern all the way up and down the ladder, jumping one jack at a time.

4. Now, repeat the pattern. But this time, jump two jacks at a time, all the way up the ladder and all the way down.

5. Then jump three jacks at a time, up and down the ladder. Continue with four and five jacks. The first player to jump all six jacks wins.

6. If you make a mistake (such as missing the tossed jackstone or knocking a "step" out of line), you lose your turn. The good news is that when it is again your turn, you can reenter the game at whichever point your error occurred.

Go for it! But be *careful!*

Match Some More Jacks

1. Little Jack Horner

A. a stand-up comedian

2. jack-o'-lantern

B. comedian and actor, *The Honeymooners*

3. Cracker Jacks

C. a flower

4. Jack Kerouac

D. used for hunting and fishing at night

5. Jackie Mason

E. a golfer

6. jack-in-the-pulpit

F. pick-up sticks

7. Jack Frost

G. . . . sat in the corner

8. "Jumpin' Jack Flash"

H. . . . went up the hill

9. jacklight

I. a spooky Halloween decoration

10. jackstraws

J. Rolling Stones song

11. Jackie Gleason

K. a classic popcorn snack

12. Jack Nicklaus

L. former Major League baseball player

13. Jack and Jill

M. First Lady, mother, book editor

14. Jackie Robinson

N. freezing weather personified

15. Jackie Onassis

O. author, *On the Road*

Answers: 1. G; 2. I; 3. K; 4. O; 5. A; 6. C; 7. N; 8. J; 9. D; 10. F; 11. B; 12. E; 13. H; 14. L; 15. M

Iguni

What you need: **12 jacks (or stones)**

In the African country of Zimbabwe, this version of *Jacks* is played with twelve smooth, round stones, all small enough to be held in one hand at once.

The game is played around the edge of a shallow hole in the ground (about two to three inches wide). So *Iguni* is another great game that's best played outside.

1. Dig a shallow hole in the ground (about two to three inches wide). Choose one of the jacks as your jackstone.

2. Evenly distribute the remaining eleven jacks around the outside edge of the hole.

3. Throw your jackstone in the air, knock one jack into the hole, then catch the jackstone before it hits the ground.

4. Repeat until all eleven jacks are in the hole.

5. Finally, toss the jackstone, use one hand to scoop all eleven jacks from the hole, then catch the jackstone with the same hand. If you don't catch the jackstone or you don't scoop out all eleven jacks, you lose your turn and start over with the eleven jacks around the hole.

6. For the second round continue the game by playing *Twosies*: Knock two jacks at a time into the hole. Then try *Threesies*.

7. Continue this pattern of play through *Elevensies*, when all the jacks must be knocked into the hole during one jackstone toss. The first player to complete *Elevensies* wins.

No Bouncing No Way

What you need: **ball, 6 jacks**

Once you've mastered *Onesies, Twosies,* and *So-Onsies,* it's time to pick up some speed. So get ready! In this game you pick up a jack and catch the ball before it bounces. Hard to do!

1. Gather the six jacks in one hand and scatter them on the playing surface with one toss.

2. With the same hand, toss the ball in the air, pick up one jack, and catch the ball before it bounces, all with the same hand.

3. With the jack still in the same hand, toss the ball in the air, transfer the jack to the other hand, and again catch the ball before it bounces.

4. Repeat steps 2 and 3 until all the jacks have been transferred to your nonthrowing hand.

5. Rescatter the jacks and proceed by twos, threes, up to and including *Sixsies*.

Five Sacks

What you need:
**5 small jacks bags
(see directions on
page 148 or use jacks)**

This popular game is from
Singapore, a small Asian
island nation, and is usually
played with small sacks of rice. *Five
Sacks* will definitely challenge your
hand-eye coordination. In some ways it
resembles one-handed juggling!

1. Scatter the five sacks.

2. Pick up one sack, toss it in the air,
pick up another sack, and catch the
tossed sack in the same hand.

3. Now it gets tricky! Throw one of the
two sacks in your hand up, pick a third

one off the ground, and catch the thrown sack, all with the same hand!

4. Repeat step 3 until you are holding all five sacks in one hand.

5. Rescatter all the sacks. Pick up one sack and toss it in the air, but this time pick up two sacks at a time.

6. Move on to *Threesies*, then *Foursies*, when you pick up all four sacks in one sweep.

Take a deep breath and get ready for the second half of *Five Sacks*.

7. Scatter the five sacks. Another player chooses the sack to be thrown (the jackstone). Arrange the four remaining sacks so that they look like this:

8. Throw the jackstone in the air, pick up the two touching sacks, and catch the thrown sack.

9. Throw the jackstone in the air, sweep up the two remaining sacks, and catch the jackstone.

10. The first player to complete both parts of Five Sacks wins. It's not easily done!

• •

Thumber: A Really Thwell Idea.

You can make any *Jacks* game more challenging by adding a "thumber." The thumber is a stone (or jack) that is placed between the thumb and first finger (in the crotch of the thumb) and held there throughout the game. Dropping or tossing the thumber means losing a turn.

• •

Over and Back

What you need: **10 small jacks (or stones)**

Over and Back can be enjoyed over and over again even without a ball.

1. Scatter the jacks. Select one of the jacks as your jackstone.

2. Toss the jackstone up in the air, pick up a jack, and catch the jackstone before it hits the ground.

3. Toss both the jackstone *and* the jack you picked up, flip your hand over, and catch them on the back of the same hand.

4. Toss them both from the back of your hand and catch them in the palm of the same hand.

5. Set the picked-up jack aside and continue in the same way until all the jacks have been picked up, one by one.

Any drops or fumbles cause you to start over. Bummer.

• • • • • • • • • • • • • • • • • • • •

Knuckle Down!

Ever wonder where the term "knuckle down"—meaning "get to work!"—comes from? It comes from the game of *Knucklebones*! Whenever a player was slow to scatter his or her bones, an opponent would yell "Knuckle down!" meaning "Hurry up and toss the knuckles down on the ground." The expression is still used regularly, and not only in *Jacks* games.

• • • • • • • • • • • • • • • • • • • •

Scatter

What you need: **6 small jacks (or stones)**

S*catter* is an incredibly challenging twist on the game of *Over and Back*.

1. Scatter (get it?) the jacks. Select one of the jacks as your jackstone. Toss the jackstone in the air, pick up another jack, and catch the jackstone before it hits the ground. Toss the jackstone and the jack you picked up and catch them on the back of your hand. Toss them both from the back of your hand and catch them in the palm of your hand.

So far this game is the same as *Over and Back*. But now, it's going to get tough—really, really tough.

2. Toss both jacks in the palm of your hand and pick up a third. Then catch the two tossed jacks. It can be done!

3. Toss all three jacks and catch them on the back of your hand.

4. Toss all three jacks and catch them in the palm of your hand. Then continue this pattern until all the jacks are picked up.

5. On the final play, all six jacks will be tossed from your palm, caught on the back of your hand, tossed from there, and caught in your palm. Wow! You can really impress your friends if you master this game.

A Fistful of Jacks

What you need: **ball, 6 jacks**

Have you noticed that a lot of *Jacks* games have you flicking, pushing, or throwing horses, eggs, or pigs into a stall, basket, or pen? Not this one. Here you're simply putting jacks on top of your fist.

1. Make a fist with your nonthrowing hand and set it on the floor.

2. Scatter the six jacks on the playing surface with one toss.

3. Throw the ball in the air, pick up a jack—now here's the tricky part—put it on top of your fist, and—hurry!—catch the ball before it bounces.

4. Leave the jack on your fist and repeat step 3 with a second jack, then a third. Balance the new jacks carefully, and don't knock any off your fist.

5. Play *Twosies, Threesies,* etc., up through *Sixsies.* And just wait until you see how difficult it'll be to keep all those jacks on your fist while you're tossing, picking, and catching!

6. The winner is the player who first completes *Sixsies.*

TruYen-TruYen

What you need: **ball, 10 chopsticks
(or straws, twigs, or pick-up sticks)**

Truyen-Truyen is a game played by
Vietnamese children and is very
similar to *Jacks*, except that it is played
with chopsticks.

1. Drop the chopsticks onto the ground;
you want them to be well separated.
Toss the ball in the air, quickly pick up
a chopstick, and catch the ball in the
same hand, on one bounce. Then
switch the stick to your nonthrowing
hand. Continue to pick up the chopsticks one by one, until all ten have
been picked up.

2. In the next round, drop the chopsticks on the ground so that they fall a
little closer together. Pick up the chop-

sticks two at a time, until all ten chop-sticks have been picked up.

3. Continue in this manner through *Tensies*.

4. Now, for the finale: When you successfully complete *Tensies*, toss the ball, tap the chopsticks on the ground three times, and catch the ball, all with the same hand.

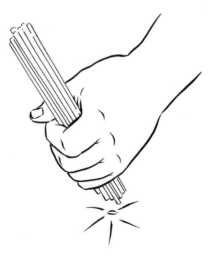

5. The first player to successfully complete all the steps is the winner.

Most Asian restaurants will give you extra wood chopsticks for free if you ask for them.

Scratches and Kisses

What you need: **ball, 10 jacks**

Have you ever had a friend (or maybe even a family member) with whom you fight, then make up, then fight, then make up? Here's a game to play with that person.

1. Gather the ten jacks in one hand and scatter them on the playing surface with one toss.

2. Toss the ball in the air, pick up one jack, and scratch it across the playing surface once, with a backward and forward movement (as if you're scratching an itch). Keep that jack in your scratching hand, then catch the ball, after only one bounce, with the same hand.

3. Transfer the jack to your other hand and continue until all ten jacks have been "scratched."

4. Rescatter and scratch by twos, then threes, and so on, all the way through *Tensies*.

5. Once you've finished the violent, scratching part of the game, make up: Instead of scratching each jack, lift it up and kiss it, then catch the tossed ball. Play all the way through *Tensies*.

And now for a really complicated emotional ride: See if you can scratch *and* kiss on each pickup!

Downcast

What you need: **ball, 6 jacks**

This is a great game for the exhausted *Jacks* player—seriously. Instead of throwing the ball in the air against the force of gravity, you throw the ball down, letting gravity do almost all the work.

1. Gather the six jacks in one hand and scatter them on the playing surface with one toss.

2. Toss the ball in the air, pick up one jack, and catch the ball, all with the same hand.

3. Then, instead of gently tossing the ball toward the sky, *throw the ball down* and transfer the jack to your other hand, while the ball bounces

once. Catch the ball with your tossing
hand and set aside the jack.

4. Proceed through *Sixsies*.

You can also play *Upcast*, a variation of *Downcast*. The only difference
is that instead of throwing the ball
down, you calmly turn the palm of your
hand and let the ball fall to the playing
surface. It's much more passive but
much more difficult since a dropped
ball doesn't bounce nearly as high as a
tossed ball.

Hamesh Avanim

What you need: **5 jacks**

In Israel, where *Hamesh Avanim* originates, the game is played with five gold-colored cubes, but you can use your jacks. As with most *Jacks* games, there are many variations of *Hamesh Avanim*. This is one of the more popular versions.

1. Gather the five jacks in one hand and scatter them on the playing surface.

2. Select one jack and place it on your palm. While you toss this jack from your palm to the back of the same hand, pick up one jack from the ground. (This is really difficult! It's a big jump in skill demand.) Continue until you've picked up all the jacks,

one by one. If you mess up, you lose
your turn.

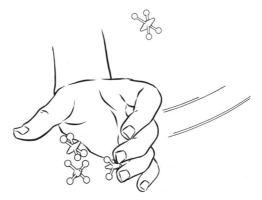

3. Now move on to *Twosies*. You must
flip and catch *two* jacks while picking
up as many as possible from the
ground.

4. Continue with this pattern up
through *Threesies* and *Foursies*. (And
you thought *Onesies* was difficult!)

5. The winner is the player who successfully completes *Foursies*.

The Whole Kit and Caboodle

What you need: **ball, 6 jacks**

This neat, short game is a fun way to end a marathon *Jacks*-playing session.

1. Place all the jacks and ball in your playing hand.

2. Toss the ball in the air, put down all the jacks, and catch the ball, all with the same hand.

3. Throw the ball in the air again, pick up all the jacks, and catch the ball in your playing hand.

Around the World

What you need: **ball, 6 jacks**

This is a great little game—an unusual but fun variation on *Onesies*.

1. Gather the six jacks in one hand and scatter them on the playing surface with one toss.

2. Toss the ball in the air, pick up one jack, and catch the ball, all with the same hand.

3. While holding the jack, toss the ball *again*, and while the ball is in the air, circle it with your hand, then catch it. Whew!

4. Set aside the jack and continue to pick up the other five in the same fashion.

5. Proceed through to *Sixsies*.

Zhua San

What you need: **9 jacks
(or stones) per player**

One version of *Jacks* played in
China—where the game of *Jacks*
is believed to have originated—is *Zhua
San* (which means "Pick Up Three"). In
this game, each player has a set of
nine stones or jacks.

1. Place all the jacks from all the players
in your throwing hand (it's really hard to
play *Zhua San* with more than three
players). Throw all the jacks in the air.
Catch as many as you can on the back
of the same hand. If you don't catch at
least two jacks, you lose your turn.

2. Toss the caught jacks, flip over your
hand, and catch just one. This will
serve as your jackstone.

If you don't catch at least one jack, you lose your turn. And if you catch more than two jacks you also lose your turn. If, by chance, you catch two jacks, the other players get to put the extra jack on the ground to add to your pick-up pile wherever they wish.

3. Throw the jackstone in the air, pick up three jacks from the ground, and catch the jackstone.

4. You've now "won" one of the four jacks in your hand. Set one of those four aside.

5. Now toss the three remaining jacks, catch one of them, and let the other two fall to the ground. The caught one is your jackstone. Toss it, pick up three more jacks, and set one aside.

6. Repeat step 5: Toss the three jacks, catch one as your jackstone, toss it, pick up three more jacks, and set one aside. Continue to repeat this pattern.

7. If you mess up and lose your turn, you still get to keep the jacks you've won. Just begin your next turn at step 3.

8. Eventually, only two jacks will be left. Toss one and pick up the other with the same hand. Catch the tossed one and set it aside.

9. Throw the last jack in the air, catch it on the back of your hand, toss it again, flip your hand, and catch it in your palm.

10. Once all the jacks are won, the winner is the player with the most jacks.

Toad in the Hole

What you need: **ball, 4 jacks (or knucklebones)**

If you take the best of *Pigs in the Pen* and combine it with the best of *Pigs over the Fence*, you end up with *Toad in the Hole*.

1. Scatter the jacks.

2. Place one hand on the ground, making an O with the tips of your forefinger and your thumb.

3. Throw the ball in the air. As the ball bounces, you must toss a jack through the O-shaped hole. Catch the ball. Make sure not to move your O-shaped hole.

4. When all the jacks have been tossed through the hole, toss the ball and pick them all up at once. The first player to do this wins.

Fivestones

What you need: **5 jacks (or cube-shaped pebbles or dice)**

The ancient game of *Knucklebones* evolved into a popular game called *Fivestones*, which is still played in many countries and is similar to *Jacks*. Players crouch on the ground and throw small cube-shaped objects into the air and catch them in an increasingly difficult series of tosses. In *Fivestones*, the basic flip is sometimes known as the "jockey."

The directions for this game of *Fivestones* use jacks, but cube-shaped pebbles or dice can also be used.

131

1. Scatter four of the jacks on the ground; keep the fifth as your jackstone.

2. Toss the jackstone in the air, sweep up one jack, and catch the jackstone in the same hand.

3. Repeat for the other three jacks, holding on to each new jack as you go, until you're holding onto all five jacks.

4. Continue on in the same manner, through *Twosies*.

5. *Threesies* is known as *The Horse and Cart*. Scoop up one jack (the horse) on the first toss, then pick up the remaining three (the cart) on the second.

6. For the final round, toss your jackstone and scoop up all four remaining jacks.

The Flying Dutchman

What you need: **ball, 6 jacks**

This is a very challenging game, almost as challenging as trying to figure out why it is called *The Flying Dutchman* and not something else, like *The Flying Canadian Kid* or *The Floating Tibetan Woman.*

1. Begin as if you're playing a simple game of *Onesies:* Scatter the jacks, toss the ball in the air, pick up a jack, and catch the ball after one bounce.

2. Now, here's the trick: Toss the ball again, toss the jack from one hand to the other,* pick up another jack, and catch the ball after only one bounce. Yikes!

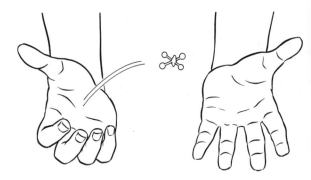

3. Continue this pattern through rounds of *Onesies*, *Twosies*, and *So-Onsies*.

4. The first player to finish *Sixsies* wins.

* This move is called "the flying Dutchman."

Abhadho

What you need: **ball, 5 jacks (or real knucklebones)***

In Tibet, where it originates, this game is most often played with the knee bones of goats. If you've misplaced your goat knee bones, that's okay—just use your jacks. Or actually, stones would seem even more appropriate, since *abha* means "many ways of grabbing" and *dho* means "stones."

1. Scatter the five jacks. Select one to be your jackstone.

2. Throw your jackstone in the air, pick up another jack from the ground, and catch the jackstone.

* See directions on page 171 for preparing knucklebones.

3. Repeat this play through *Onesies* and *Twosies*.

4. Here's the tricky Tibetan twist: When you get to *Threesies*, an opponent determines which three jacks you must pick up. You'll be surprised at what a change in the flow of the game this rule makes! Once you've picked up the three jacks, toss your jackstone and pick up the remaining jack to end the *Threesies* round.

5. Play *Foursies* as usual.

6. Finally, toss all five jacks in the air and catch them on the back of your hand.

7. The first player to complete this final step wins the game.

One-Handed Jack Juggling

What you need: **ball, 6 jacks**

Have you ever seen those people who juggle bowling balls, burning torches, and scary-looking knives? Master this game and you too can be on your way to an exciting career as a street performer! *One-Handed Jack Juggling* is a game for the more experienced *Jacks* player. It requires great hand-eye coordination, superb timing, and lightning speed. But don't be intimidated—you can master it with practice.

1. Scatter your jacks.

2. Toss the ball in the air, pick up a jack, and catch the ball, all with the same hand.

3. Toss the ball again and—here's the tricky part—toss the *jack* that's in your hand, pick up a *new* jack, catch the *thrown* jack, and then catch the ball before it bounces. Wow!

Continue through *Onesies*, always throwing just one jack, and only using one hand.

4. Continue through the terrible *Twosies*. Now you'll be tossing the ball, tossing two jacks, picking up two more jacks, catching the two tossed jacks, and then catching the ball before it bounces.

5. Continue this pattern all the way through to the completion of *Sixsies* (if you can!). You can see why *One-Handed Jack Juggling* is for the more experienced player. Master this game and your reputation as a "Jackspert" will be secure.

For an extra challenge, try juggling with your right hand if you're left-handed and with your left hand if you're right-handed.

• • • • • • • • • • • • • • • • • • • •

Jackstraws

The game called jackstraws uses sticks or straws and is played like the game of pick-up sticks. It has nothing to do with Jacks.

• • • • • • • • • • • • • • • • • • • •

Knucklebones: Mauritius Style

What you need: **1 ball (or jackstone), 10 jacks (or stones) per player**

Mauritius is a mountainous island in the Indian Ocean. This version of *Knucklebones* is a favorite in this former British republic because of its unique "three" twist that changes the strategy and rhythm of the more traditional game. Ever heard the expression "Three's a crowd"?

1. Scatter your ten jacks.

2. Toss the ball, pick up as many jacks as possible and catch the ball, all with the same hand.

3. Here's the twist: When picking up

the jacks, you must avoid multiples of three. That's right, three. You cannot pick up three jacks, or leave three jacks on the ground.

So, if there are seven jacks on the ground you can pick up two, five, or seven, but not one, three, four, or six. Or if there are ten jacks on the ground, you can't pick up seven and leave three (or vice versa), or pick up six and leave four (or vice versa, because six is a multiple of three), or pick up one and leave nine.

As always, you cannot touch or move any jacks except those you're picking up.

Set aside all of the picked-up jacks as winnings.

4. Continue picking up jacks and laying them aside until you miss. If you end up winning all of your own jacks, it becomes the next player's turn.

5. If you make a mistake, leave your unplayed jacks where they are; the next player now has a chance to win them. Your opponents must first play their own jacks; they cannot start winning your jacks until they've picked up all of their own.

6. The winner is the player who has everybody's jacks, or whoever has the most jacks when you stop playing (when the end-of-recess bell rings, for instance).

Maakgep

What you need: **5 jacks (or stones)**

Maakgep (pronounced MOCK-gepp, with a hard *g* sound, as in "goose") is a popular game in the Asian nation of Thailand. Thailand means "land of the free," so if you play *Maakgep* with stones, as they do in Thailand, the cost of this game would also be free.

1. First, decide on the winning point total you're aiming for; fifteen works well.

2. Scatter the five jacks. Choose one as your jackstone.

3. Toss the jackstone, pick up one jack, and put the picked-up jack aside.

4. Once the four jacks are picked up and put aside, gather all *five* jacks in your palm, throw them in the air, and catch them on the back of the same hand. Count how many you catch; this becomes your score for that round.

5. Keep playing through *Twosies*, *Threesies*, and *Foursies*, noting the score at the end of each round.

6. The winner is the first person to score fifteen points (or whatever your predetermined point goal was). If you

get through *Foursies* and nobody has reached the winning score, start over with *Onesies*.

If you find that *Maakgep* is too easy, either raise the final point goal or try to keep each picked-up jack in your throwing hand while you pick up the rest.

• •

Ancient History

Tropa is the name of another game that the ancient Greeks played with knucklebones. In *Tropa*, the players would try to toss the knucklebones into a narrow-necked jar. The winner was the person who landed the most bones in the jar.

• •

CHAPTER 4

Other *Jacks* Stuff

✣ ✣ ✣

One of the great things about *Jacks* is that they are so simple, yet so incredibly versatile. And with just a little bit of imagination, you can enjoy them in all sorts of cool ways. This chapter shares some ideas for other ways to enjoy your jacks: sew a set of jacks sacks, cook up your own knucklebones, sponsor a *Jacks* tournament, perform jacks magic, or party with jacks. You can even impress your teacher and classmates with a *Jacks* social studies project. Just combine your jacks and your imagination, and have fun!

HOW TO MAKE YOUR OWN JACKS BAGS

Jacks bags are easy and fun to make from fabric scraps you have around the house. A lightweight fabric, such as cotton gingham, works best.

What you need:

a pen or pencil

a piece of cardboard, large enough to have a 3$\frac{1}{2}$-inch diameter circle drawn on it

scissors

a small piece of fabric to cut into a 3$\frac{1}{2}$-inch diameter circle (this will be your jackstone)

a larger piece of fabric, of another color, big enough so that you can cut out eight 3$\frac{1}{2}$-inch diameter circles

uncooked rice

measuring spoon

string or narrow ribbon

1. Using a pen or pencil, draw a circle about 3½ inches in diameter onto your cardboard (a small bowl of the right size may help you trace the circle). Cut out the circle.

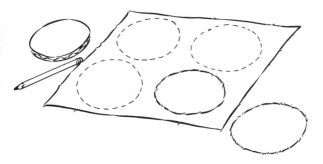

2. Using the cardboard circle as a guide, trace one circle onto the jack-stone fabric.

3. Trace eight circles onto the larger piece of fabric.

4. Cut out the nine circles. Place the fabric, *right side down*, onto your work surface. Place about ¹/₂ teaspoon of rice in the center of each cloth circle. Gather the sides of the fabric around the rice, and tie closed with the string or ribbon.

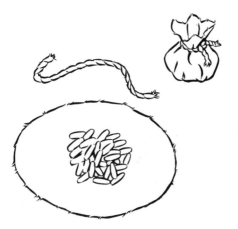

PARTY!

Are you bored with standard sleepovers and run-of-the-mill parties? Then how about a *Jacks* party? Here's your chance to be a party trendsetter.

• All your guests receive their own copy of this book or a set of jacks as they arrive (that way everybody has won a prize before the party has even started!).

• Make a tape of "jack" songs (like "Jumpin' Jack Flash" and "Hit the Road, Jack") and play it throughout the party.

• Serve Cracker Jacks, Jax Cheese Puffs, Apple Jacks, flapjacks, or grilled Monterey Jack cheese sandwiches.

• Play five or six of the games from this book and award the winners more prizes (like a jack-in-the-box) or privileges (like "first-in-line" at the make-your-own-sundae table).

• Do a little research at the library so that when you play one of the international games, you can wear clothing unique to a country's culture, or use words from their language.

Just remember, it's thinking like this that got Martha Stewart started.

AN A+ #1 SOCIAL STUDIES PROJECT

The next time you have to do a school project, throw away that old poster board and consider using the game of *Jacks* as your topic. It's different, it's fun, and it's educational. Teachers really *love* that combination. And your class-mates will thank you for a fun and interesting presentation.

You might start by reading through this book for some ideas. You could include the history of *Jacks*, *Jacks* in other cultures, and your favorite variations of the game. Your project presentation could include a written report, a set of jacks, a set of homemade knuckle-bones, and a set of jacks bags you made yourself. You could include a large map of the world and show all the places where the game is played and what the game is called in each country. (The bibliography at the back of this book lists many other other books that would be helpful in your research.) And best of all, you could get everybody, including your teacher, to play some of the games in this book!

Then sit back and enjoy the ride to the High Honor Roll (if you're not there already).

ORGANIZE A SCHOOL OR NEIGHBORHOOD *JACKS* TOURNAMENT

Few things are as fun and energizing as a bit of friendly competition; however, as a rule, few competitive activities seem fair to most participants. *Jacks* is the exception to that rule. You don't have to be musical or athletic to enjoy *Jacks* and neither age nor physical fitness is an issue, as in wrestling or Roller Derby. A seven-year-old, a twenty-seven-year-old, and a fifty-seven-year-old can be very evenly matched competitors.

So how about organizing a *Jacks* tournament? Which *Jacks* games should be played? Who should be included? How many jacks will you use? It's really up to you, the organizer. Here are a few ideas:

• Pick one game, let's say *Tensies*, and that's what everybody has to play. Or, set it up so that more experienced players participate in a more difficult game while new players enjoy an easier game.

• Turn your tournament into a charity fund-raiser by charging a small entry fee. Or, participants could seek a sponsor like a neighborhood business, and you could charge a higher entry fee.

• Organize a neighborhood tournament to raise money for playground repairs or to welcome new neighbors.

• Have a school tournament, or make your tournament part of an orientation day for new students.

• Offer one grand prize or several prizes so that the runner-up players are also rewarded.

• Create a tournament scorecard. For example, if you have seven participants, your tournament scorecard would look something like this:

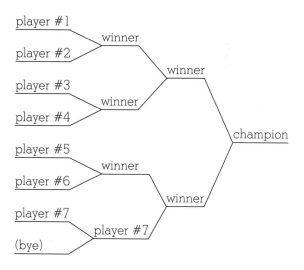

Just remember, the very best way to enjoy a tournament is not to make it *just your own*, but to organize it with friends and get as many people involved as possible.

OTHER FUN THINGS TO DO WITH JACKS

Snatch a Jack

Raise your right elbow (or your left, if you're left-handed) until your forearm is parallel to the floor and your right hand is palm up beside your right ear. Place a jack on top of your elbow and then, by dropping your elbow, suddenly catch the jack in your right hand. Once you've mastered one jack, you can add more!

Musical Jacks

All players march barefoot to music around a circle of jacks that contains

one less jack than the number of players. When the music stops, the players try to pick up a jack with their feet. The person without a jack is out.

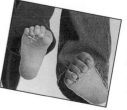

Jacks Hat Toss

Place an upside-down hat in the center of the floor. Standing several feet away, toss the jacks into the hat. The person who tosses the most jacks into the hat wins.

Jack's Face

You can enjoy *Jack's Face* by yourself, or as a game with two players.

1. Arrange eight jacks like a face, on the floor: two for the eyes, one for the nose, and five for the mouth.

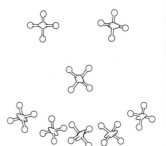

2. On the back of your playing hand, rest a ninth jack.

3. The challenge is to pick up the eight jacks with your playing hand, one by one, without the ninth jack falling off your hand. When done, your hand will be holding eight jacks with a ninth resting on top.

4. The winner is the first to complete all of the steps without an error.

Jack Trickery

What you need: **1 jack, lots of time to practice**

This is a neat trick. You're going to lose a jack and then seem to find it behind somebody else's ear.

1. Using your left hand, pinch a jack between your first two fingers and your thumb. With the back of your hand toward an audience, display the jack, keeping all your fingers close together.

2. Pretend to take the jack into your right hand by encircling the jack with the fingers of your right hand. Remember, keep the back of your hands toward the audience.

But what you're really going to do is let the jack drop into your left palm and then contract your left hand just a bit to hold the jack. At the same moment, close your right hand into a fist. The audience will assume the jack is in your closed right hand and not in your slightly contracted left hand.

Practice this essential step in front of a mirror (this gives you the audience's view of your hands).

3. Now slowly extend your fisted right hand out to the audience. Follow the fist with your eyes. This will encourage the audience to do the same. At the same time, casually let your left hand fall to your side.

4. Tell your audience that you know something really weird about jacks, that "jacks like noise, lots of noise. That's why they call it a *jack*hammer." Tell the audience to watch as the jack reacts to your scream.

5. Get ready, take a deep breath, and scream, "JACK!" Open up your right hand (it'll be empty, of course). Act stunned, devastated, and confused. Say something like, "Gee, I don't know what went wrong. I thought jacks loved noises. This doesn't make sense. Where is it? What happened? This is awful. I've got find it."

6. Go looking for your jack. Walk near your audience. Look all around them, saying "Where did it go?"

7. Suddenly stop, hesitate, and then state that you think you might see it. Carefully look around a person's head before announcing that yes, indeed, you have found the jack. Reach behind the person's ear with your left hand and pull out the jack (which you've carefully kept cupped in your left hand).

8. Conclude by saying, "But of course, that's it! Jacks love noises. What better place for a jack to hang out than next to an ear where *everything* is heard."

"THIS OLD MAN"

The song "This Old Man" was inspired by an early Irish version of *Jacks*. The game was played with ten stones, thus ten verses. Because the song has been around for so long, the verses may vary. Here's one version; sing it as you play *Onesies*—a verse for every jack you pick up.

This old man
He played one.
He played nick nack on my drum.
With a nick nack paddy whack
Give the dog a bone
This old man came rolling home.

This old man
He played two.
He played nick nack on my shoe.
With a nick nack paddy whack
Give the dog a bone
This old man came rolling home.

This old man
He played three.
He played nick nack on my knee.
With a nick nack paddy whack
Give the dog a bone
This old man came rolling home.

This old man
He played four.
He played nick nack on my door.
With a nick nack paddy whack
Give the dog a bone
This old man came rolling home.

This old man
He played five.
He played nick nack on my hide.
With a nick nack paddy whack
Give the dog a bone
This old man came rolling home.

This old man
He played six.
He played nick nack on my sticks.

With a nick nack paddy whack
Give the dog a bone
This old man came rolling home.

This old man
He played seven.
He played nick nack up in heaven.
With a nick nack paddy whack
Give the dog a bone
This old man came rolling home.

This old man
He played eight.
He played nick nack on my gate.
With a nick nack paddy whack
Give the dog a bone
This old man came rolling home.

This old man
He played nine.
He played nick nack on my spine.
With a nick nack paddy whack
Give the dog a bone
This old man came rolling home.

This old man
He played ten.
He played nick nack over again.
With a nick nack paddy whack
Give the dog a bone
This old man came rolling home.

HOW TO MAKE YOUR OWN KNUCKLEBONES

This makes a great school project!

What you need:

$\frac{1}{2}$ **cup flour**
$\frac{1}{4}$ **cup salt**
mixing bowl and spoon
$\frac{1}{4}$ **cup cold water**
Popsicle stick or coffee stirrer
Crayon with a sharpened point
An adult (to bake them for you)
Cookie sheet

1. Mix the flour and salt together in a mixing bowl, then add the water.

2. Stir the mixture until the dough comes cleanly away from the sides of the bowl.

3. Take a heaping teaspoon of the dough and roll it in the palms of your hands, making a ball about half the size of your jacks ball.

4. Put the dough on a flat surface and flatten it into a circular disk about ½ inch thick.

5. Holding the flattened sides with your thumb and forefinger, make two grooves in the dough about three-fourths of the way around with a Popsicle stick or coffee stirrer.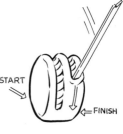

START

FINISH

6. Flatten the untouched part into a base, so that the knucklebone is freestanding.

7. With the tip of a crayon, make four indentations on the base, as shown.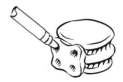

8. Ask an adult to bake the knucklebones on a cookie sheet at 275°F for one hour.

Allow the knucklebones to cool before you use them.

REAL KNUCKLEBONES: HOW TO COOK YOUR OWN OSSELETS

Osselets, which are made from lamb, veal, or beef knuckles, can be used in place of jacks for many games.

To make your own, go to your butcher or the meat counter of your grocery store and buy enough beef or lamb knucklebones to make a set of ten. (Depending on where you live, the meat counter of your neighborhood grocery store may not have knucklebones, so you might have to find a butcher shop.)

Ask an ADULT to boil them until all the meat falls off. When they're cool and dry, you'll have osselets. Here is a photo of osselets prepared by the author.

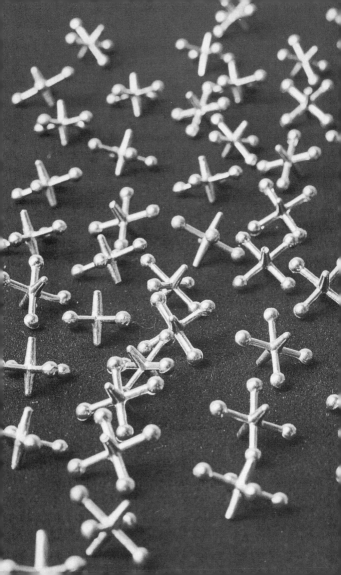

INDEX OF GAMES

BIBLIOGRAPHY

Culin, Stewart. *Korean Games: With Notes on the Corresponding Games of China and Japan*. Mineola, NY: Dover Publications, 1991.

Erlbach, Arlene. *Sidewalk Games Around the World*. Brookfield, CT: The Millbrook Press, 1997.

Grunfelt, Frederic V., ed. *Games of the World: How to Make Them, How to Play Them, How They Came to Be*. NY: Holt, Rinehart and Winston, 1975.

Hindman, Darwin A. *The Complete Book of Games and Stunts*. Englewood Cliffs, NJ: Prentice-Hall, 1956.

Johnson, June. *The Outdoor-Indoor Fun Book*. NY: Harper & Brothers, 1961.

The Klutz Book of Jacks. Palo Alto, CA: Klutz Press, 1988.

"Knuckle Bones." *Cricket Magazine*, November 1990.

Lankford, Mary D. *Jacks Around the World*. NY: Morrow Junior Books, 1996.

Maguire, Jack. *Hopscotch, Hangman, Hot Potato, & Ha, Ha, Ha: A Rulebook of Children's Games*. NY: Prentice-Hall Press, 1990.

Mohr, Merilyn Simonds. *The Games Treasury: More Than 300 Indoor and Outdoor Favorites*